Calming the Angry Dragon within

Teaching Muslim Kids About Anger Management & How to Deal With Their Feelings & Emotions From the Quran and Hadith

BY THE SINCERE SEEKER KIDS COLLECTION

Once upon a time, in a far-off land, there lived a little boy named Sam. Sam was a lovely boy but had an issue with not being able to control his emotions. Whenever something small upset him, he would often transform into a scary dragon and lash out at his family and friends. He would breathe fire and stomp his feet whenever he didn't get his way.

This would often scare the people around him. His friends distanced themselves from him because they feared dragons, and his little sister, Raya, who was closest to him, was affected the most by his behavior. Raya stopped going to Sam's room because she didn't like seeing him that way. When he would have an outburst, Raya would run to her room feeling scared and helpless. Sam soon found himself lonely and sad.

Sam's parents loved him very much and tried everything they could to help him control his anger and not turn into a dragon, from taking him to the school counselor to reading books on anger, but nothing seemed to work.

One day, things got really bad. Sam got angry at little Raya because she accidentally stepped on his homework. Sam's anger had reached a boiling point. He grew wings, giant claws, and a tail. He transformed into a dragon and lashed out at his sister, saying terrible things and breaking his mom's beautiful vase. His sister was so hurt that she couldn't even look at him, so she ran to her room. All she could think about is how anger had affected Sam and her family and what her mom would feel once she found out about her beautiful vase.

"I don't care, I'm going to my room," said dragon Sam as he ran to his room, slamming the door with his tail.

He sat on his bed, thinking about what had just happened and regretting saying what he just said. Sam was at his lowest point. He raised his head and pointed his palms up, crying to Allah: "I didn't mean what I said. I don't know why this happens to me. I don't like turning into a dragon. I don't like hurting and scaring my family and friends. Please help me, Allah. You can help anyone because you can do anything!"

Sam lay in his bed with his eyes closed. Suddenly, he heard a knock on his bedroom window. He opened it and saw a beautiful purple raven.

"Who are you?" asked Sam.

"My name is Violet. I was sent to you by Allah to help you control your emotions and prevent you from turning into a scary dragon," said Violet.

"Now I need you to go back to bed and close your eyes again," said Violet.

Sam walked over to his bed and lay down, closing his eyes.

Sam woke up to find himself in a blue room. "Where am I?" asked Sam.

Violet appeared from the corner and said, "That's not important right now, Sam. You need to know that anger is a big feeling that comes from inside and sometimes results from the desire for revenge. Although anger is a natural feeling, it can have severe and harmful effects on you and the people in your life if you allow it to control you, turning you into a dragon.

For this reason, Allah has a great deal to say about the negative emotion of anger you sometimes feel. Allah teaches us its dangers, how to control it, and the rewards for those who don't let it take over them." said the purple raven.

Why does anger happen to me?" asked Sam.

"We sometimes feel angry when we don't get what we want, when things don't go our way, when something isn't fair, or when asked to do something we don't want to do. Sometimes, anger comes from inflation of our egos. We should always work on humbling ourselves." said the raven.

"When I turn into a dragon, I feel I have strength, but I say things I don't mean in a loud voice only to later regret it. I really wish I stop doing that," said Sam.

"It's important that you realize anger and speaking up in a loud matter is a weakness, not strength. Anger is a fire sparked from inside that hurts you and the others around you. Our Prophet Muhammad PBUH stated, *"The strong man is not one who overpowers others well, but the strong man controls himself when he is in a fit of rage."*

"My friends have stopped hanging out with me, and my little sister is scared of me," said Sam, with sadness on his face as he looks down.

"Anger can cause a lot of problems. Anger is often the root cause of many problems with family and friends. Anger can ruin loving relationships that took years to build. Anger can also ruin your health, education, job, money, and more!" said the wise raven.

"Have a seat, Sam," said Violet.

"Satan is our enemy, and uncontrolled anger comes from Satan. It is one of the tools he uses to cause problems. Whenever there is a situation in which you possibly feel angry, Satan jumps into the opportunity, whispering in your ears, enticing you to act without thinking, while making things bigger than they really are. When you are in a situation that starts to anger you, remove yourself from that situation and immediately say: *I seek Refuge with Allah from Satan* (أَعُوذُ بِاللَّهِ مِنَ الشَّيْطَانِ) as our Prophet Muhammad, PBUH, taught us. If you are upset and standing, you should sit down; if you are sitting, you should lie down.

"Satan doesn't sound very nice," said Sam.

"That's right, he is not friendly at all. Our Prophet Muhammad, PBUH, says that "...*Anger comes from the devil, the devil was created of fire, and fire is extinguished only with water; so when one of you becomes angry, he should perform wudu (ablution).* So Sam, whenever you are angry or in an argument or debate with someone, go make wudu to cool off, following your Prophet PBUH's advice. Practice letting go of arguments. Our Prophet Muhammad, PBUH, stated, *I promise a house in the outskirts of Paradise to the one who leaves arguing even if he's right.* Arguing is not worth it. Leave it, and you'll get a house in Paradise from Allah, advised the raven.

"You should realize that whatever you get in this world is only temporary and insignificant compared to what you will have in the next world. If you lose something or do not get what you want, it's okay. It's not worth being angry about. Our Prophet Muhammad, PBUH, never got angry about something in this world," said the raven.

"And you know what, Sam?" asked the raven.

"What? replies Sam.

"I know what you shouted to your sister when she stepped on your homework. It was not nice. Bad words can hurt people; once you say them, they cannot be taken back. Our Prophet Muhammad, PBUH, stated, *"When you are angry, be silent."* This prevents you from saying something you will later regret.

"I know I was wrong. I shouldn't have said it. I will apologize to my sister. I will not turn into a dragon anymore! "said Sam with a spark of motivation."

Before I get you back to your room, I need to tell you a couple more things you should know that will help you," said the purple raven.

"Okay, I'm listening, Violet," said Sam.

"We know from our Creator, Allah, and from our Prophet, Muhammad PBUH, of the benefits and rewards you would get if you control your anger and do not act on it. The Holy Quran teaches us that righteous individuals who cover up their anger, control it, and forgive others are promised the highest form of Jannah. Feeling angry inside is okay; you just can't act upon that anger. Controlling anger is a sign of righteousness," said the purple raven.

"I will need to work hard to control my anger, so I can be rewarded a house in paradise," said Sam.

"I think you are ready to return. You learned a lot. Go lie down on that bed made of clouds in the corner and close your eyes," said Violet. Sam walked to the bed, lay down, and closed his eyes.

Sam opened his eyes and found himself back in his room. Violet was not there, and the window was closed. Sam stood up and went downstairs, where his parents and sister were sitting. Sam apologized to his family and told them what he had learned from Violet.

"I don't know who Violet is, but Violet sounds like one wise purple raven," said Sam's dad.

The next day Sam was in class, and one of his classmates accidentally spilled water all over his backpack. Sam stood up and was about to turn into a dragon, but then he remembered what he had learned from Violet. He took a deep breath and said, *I seek Refuge with Allah from Satan* (أَعُوذُ بِاللَّهِ مِنَ الشَّيْطَانِ). He then sat down and told his classmate that it's okay; accidents happen. He raised his hand and asked his teacher if he could go to the restroom.

He made wudu in the bathroom and looked at himself in the mirror. He was himself again! He was Sam. He didn't grow wings, nor did he have giant claws and a tail. He was not a dragon. He was Sam.

He smiled.

The End.

Printed in Great Britain
by Amazon

39733859R00023